THE DUEL

BETWEEN

FRANCE AND GERMANY,

WITH

ITS LESSON TO CIVILIZATION.

LECTURE

BY

CHARLES SUMNER.

> "For when kings make war,
> No law betwixt two sovereigns can decide,
> But that of arms, where fortune is the judge,
> Soldiers the lawyers, and the bar the field."
> — DRYDEN.

BOSTON:
LEE AND SHEPARD.
1871.

UNIVERSITY PRESS: WELCH, BIGELOW, & CO.,
CAMBRIDGE.

LECTURE.

MR. PRESIDENT, — I am to speak of the Duel between France and Germany, with its Lesson to Civilization. In calling the terrible war now waging a duel, I might content myself with classical authority, *duellum* being a well-known Latin word for war. The historian Livy makes a Roman declare that affairs are to be settled " by a pure and pious duel " ; the dramatist Plautus has a character in one of his plays who obtains great riches " by the duelling art," meaning the Art of War ; and Horace, the exquisite master of language, hails the age of Augustus with the Temple of Janus closed and " free from duels," meaning at peace, for then only was that famous temple shut.

WAR UNDER THE LAW OF NATIONS A DUEL.

But no classical authority is needed for this designation. War, as conducted under International Law, between two organized nations, is in all respects a duel, according to the just signification of this word, differing from that between two individuals only in the number of combatants. The variance is of proportion merely, each nation being an individual who appeals to the sword as Arbiter, and in each case the combat is subject to rules constituting a code by which the two parties are bound. For long years before civilization prevailed, the code governing the duel between individuals was as fixed and minute as that which governs the larger duel between nations, and the duel itself was simply a mode of deciding questions between individuals. In presenting this comparison I expose myself to criticism only from those who have not considered this interesting subject in the light of history and of reason. The parallel is complete. Modern war is the Duel of the Dark Ages, magnified, amplified, extended so as to embrace nations; nor is it any less a duel, because the combat is quickened and sustained by the energies of self-defence, or because, when a champion falls and lies on the ground, he is brutally treated. An authentic instance illustrates such a duel; and I bring before you the very pink of chivalry, the Chevalier Bayard, the knight without fear and without reproach, who, after combat in a chosen field, succeeded by a feint in driving his weapon four inches deep into the throat of his adversary, and then, rolling with him, gasping and struggling, on the ground, thrust his dagger into the nostrils of the fallen victim, exclaiming, "Surrender, or you are a dead man," — a speech which seemed superfluous, for the second cried out, "He is dead; you have conquered." Then did Bayard, brightest among the sons of war, drag his dead enemy from the field, crying, "Have I done enough?" Now, because the brave knight saw fit to do these things, the combat was not changed in original character. It was a duel at the beginning and at the end. Indeed, the brutality with which it closed was the natural incident of a duel. A combat once begun opens the way to violence, and the conqueror too often surrenders to the Evil Spirit, as Bayard, in his unworthy barbarism.

In likening war between nations to the duel, I follow not only reason, but authority also. No better lawyer can be named in the long history of the English bar than John Selden, whose learning was equalled only by his large intelligence. In those conversations which, under the name of Table-Talk, continue still to instruct, the wise counsellor, after saying that the Church allowed the duel anciently, and that in the public liturgies there were prayers appointed for duellists, keenly inquires, "But whether is this lawful?" And then he answers, "If you grant any war lawful, I make no doubt but to convince it." Selden regarded the simple duel and the larger war as governed by the same rule. Of course the exercise of force in the suppression of rebellion, or in the maintenance of laws, stands on a different principle, being in its nature a constabulary proceeding, which cannot be confounded with the duel. But my object is not to question the lawfulness of war; I would simply present an image, enabling you to see the existing war in its true character.

The duel in its simplest form is between two individuals. In early ages it was known sometimes as the Judicial Combat and sometimes as Trial by Battle. Not only points of honor, but titles to land, grave questions of law, and even the subtilties of theology, were referred to this arbitrament, — just as now kindred issues between nations are referred to Trial by Battle; and the early rules governing the duel are reproduced in the Laws of War established by nations to govern the great Trial by Battle. Ascending from the individual to corporations, guilds, villages, towns, counties, provinces, we find that for a long period each of these bodies exercised what was called "the right of war." The history of France and Germany shows how reluctantly this mode of trial yielded to the forms of reason and order. France, earlier than Germany, ordained "trial by proofs," and eliminated the duel from judicial proceedings, this important step being followed by the amalgamation of discordant provinces in the powerful unity of the Nation, so that Brittany and Normandy, Franche-Comté and Burgundy, Provence and Dauphiny, Gascony and Languedoc, became the United States of France, or, if you please, France. In Germany the change was slower; and here the duel exhibits its most curious instances. Not only feudal chiefs, but associations of tradesmen and of domestics sent defiance to each other, and sometimes to whole cities, on pretences trivial as those which have been the occasion of defiance from nation to nation. There still remain to us Declarations of War by a lord of Prauenstein against the free city of Frankfort, because a young lady of the city refused to dance with his uncle, — by the baker and domestics of the Margrave of Baden against Eslingen, Reutlingen, and other imperial cities, — by the baker of the Count Palatine Louis against the cities of Augsburg, Ulm, and Rottweil, — by the shoe-blacks of the University of Leipzig against the provost and other members, — and by the cook of Eppstein, with his scullions, dairy-maids, and dishwashers, against Otho, Count of Solms. This prevalence of the duel aroused the Emperor Maximilian, who, at the Diet of Worms, put forth an ordinance abolishing the right or liberty of Private War, and instituting a Supreme Tribunal for the determination of controversies without appeal to the duel, and the whole long list of duellists, whether corporate or individual, including nobles, bakers, shoe-blacks, and cooks, were brought under its pacific rule. Unhappily the beneficent reform stopped half-way, and here Germany was less fortunate than France. The great provinces were left in the enjoyment of a barbarous independence, with the "right" to fight each other. The duel continued their established Arbiter, until at last, in 1815, by the Act of Union constituting the Confederation or United States of Germany, each sovereignty gave up the right of war with its confederates, setting an example to the larger nations. The terms of this important stipulation, marking a stage in German unity, were as follows : " The members further bind themselves under no pretext to declare war against one another, or to pursue their mutual differences by force of arms, but engage to submit them to the Diet." Better words could not be found for the United States of Europe in the establishment of that Great Era when the duel shall cease to be the recognized Arbiter of Nations.

With this exposition, which I hope is not too long, it is easy to see how completely a war between two nations is a duel, — and, yet further, how essential it is to that assured peace which civilization requires, that the duel, which is no longer tolerated as Arbiter between individuals, between towns, between counties, between provinces, should cease to be tolerated as such between nations. Take our own country, for instance. In a controversy between towns, the local law provides a judicial tribunal; so also in a controversy between counties. Ascending still higher, suppose a controversy between two States of our Union; the National Constitution establishes a judicial tribunal, being the Supreme Court of the United States. But at the next stage there is a change. Let the controversy arise between two nations, and the Supreme Law, which is the Law of Nations, establishes, not a judicial tribunal, but the duel, as Arbiter. What is true of our country is true of other countries where civilization has a foothold, and especially of France and Germany. The duel, though abolished as Arbiter at home, is continued as Arbiter abroad. And since it is recognized by International Law and subjected to a code, it is in all respects an Institution. War is an Institution sanctioned by International Law, as Slavery, wherever it exists, is an Institution sanctioned by Municipal Law. But this institution is nothing but the duel of the Dark Ages, prolonged into this generation, and showing itself in portentous barbarism.

WHY THIS PARALLEL NOW?

Therefore am I right when I call the existing combat between France and Germany a duel. I beg you to believe that I do this with no idle purpose of illustration or criticism, but because I would prepare the way for a proper comprehension of the remedy to be applied. How can this terrible controversy be adjusted? I see no practical method, which shall reconcile the sensibilities of France with the guaranties due to Germany, short of a radical change in the War System itself. That security for the Future, which Germany may justly exact, can be obtained in no way so well as by the disarmament of France; to be followed naturally by the disarmament of other nations, and the substitution of some peaceful tribunal for the existing Trial by Battle. Any dismemberment, or curtailment of territory, will be poor and inadequate, for it will leave behind a perpetual sting. Something better must be done.

SUDDENNESS OF THIS WAR.

Never in history has so great a calamity descended so suddenly upon the Human Family, unless we except the earthquake toppling down cities and submerging a whole coast in a single night. But how small all that has ensued from any such convulsion, compared with the desolation and destruction already produced by this war! From the first murmur to the outbreak was a brief moment of time, as between the flash of lightning and the bursting of the thunder.

At the beginning of July there was peace without suspicion of interruption. The Legislative Body had just discussed a proposition for the reduction of the annual army contingent. At Berlin the Parliament was not in session. Count Bismarck was at his country home in Pomerania, the King enjoying himself at Ems. How sudden and unexpected the change will appear from an illustrative circumstance. M. Prévost-Paradol, of rare talent and unhappy destiny, newly appointed Minister to the United States, embarked at Havre on the 1st of July, and reached Washington on the evening of the 14th of July. He assured me that when he left France there was no talk or thought of war. During his brief summer voyage the whole startling event had begun and culminated. The Prince Leopold Hohenzollern-Sigmaringen being invited to become candidate for the throne of Spain, France promptly sent her defiance to Prussia, followed a few days later by formal

Declaration of War. The Minister was oppressed by the grave tidings coming upon him so unprepared, and sought relief in self-slaughter, being the first victim of the war. Everything moved with a rapidity borrowed from the new forces supplied by human invention, and the gates of war swung wide open.

CHALLENGE TO PRUSSIA.

A few incidents exhibit this movement. It was on the 30th of June, while discussing the proposed reduction of the army, that Émile Ollivier, the Prime Minister, said openly : " The Government has no kind of anxiety ; at no epoch was the maintenance of peace more assured ; whatever side you look, you see no irritating question." In the same debate Garnier-Pagès, the consistent Republican, and now a member of the Provisional Government, after asking "Why these armaments?" cried out : " Disarm without waiting for others: this is practical. Let the people be relieved from the taxes which crush them, and from the heaviest of all, the tax of blood." The candidature of Prince Leopold seems to have become known at Paris on the 5th of July. On the next day the Duc de Gramont, of a family famous in scandalous history, Minister of Foreign Affairs, hurries to the tribune with defiance on his lips. After declaring for the Cabinet that no Foreign Power could be suffered, by placing one of its princes on the throne of Charles the Fifth, to derange the balance of power in Europe, and put in peril the interests and the honor of France, he concludes by saying, in ominous words, that, "strong in your support, gentlemen, and in that of the nation, we shall know how to fulfil our duty without hesitation and without weakness." This defiance was followed by what is called in the report, "general and prolonged movement, — repeated applause"; and here was the first stage in the duel. Its character was recognized at once in the Chamber. Garnier-Pagès exclaimed in words worthy of memory : " It is dynastic questions which trouble the peace of Europe. The people have reason only to love and aid each other." Though short, better than many long speeches. Crémieux, an associate in the Provisional Government of 1848, insisted that the utterance of the Minister was " a menace of war"; and Emmanuel Arago, son of the great Republican astronomer and mathematician, said that the Minister "had declared war." These patriotic representatives were not mistaken. The speech made peace difficult, if not impossible. It was a challenge to Prussia.

COMEDY.

Europe watched with dismay as the gauntlet was thus rudely flung down, while on this side of the Atlantic, where France and Germany commingle in the enjoyment of our equal citizenship, the interest was intense. Morning and evening the telegraph made us all partakers of the hopes and fears agitating the world. Too soon it was apparent that the exigence of France would not be satisfied, while already her preparations for war were undisguised. At all the naval stations, from Toulon to Cherbourg, the greatest activity prevailed. Marshal McMahon was recalled from Algeria, and transports were made ready to bring back the troops from that colony. Meanwhile the consent of the King of Prussia to the candidature of Prince Leopold was withdrawn, and he ceased to be a candidate. But this was not enough. The King was asked to promise that the candidature should in no event hereafter be renewed, which he declined to do, reserving to himself the liberty of consulting circumstances. This requirement was the more offensive, inasmuch as it was addressed exclusively to Prussia while nothing was said to Spain, the principal in the business. Then ensued an incident, proper for comedy, if it had not become the declared cause of tragedy. The French Ambassador, Count Benedetti, following the King to Ems, his favorite watering-place, pressed him in successive interviews, when at last his Majesty, after ascertaining that he had come a third time on the same errand, let him know, with perfect politeness, by an adjutant in attendance, that he had nothing further for him, and this refusal to receive the ambassador was promptly communicated by telegraph for the information especially of the different German governments.

PRETEXT OF THE TELEGRAM.

These simple facts, insufficient for the slightest quarrel, intolerable in the pettiness of the issue disclosed, and monstrous as reason for war between two civilized nations, became the welcome pretext. Swiftly, and with ill-disguised alacrity, the French Cabinet took the next step in the duel. On the 15th of July the Prime Minister read from the tribune a manifesto, setting forth the griefs of France, being, first, the refusal of the Prussian King to promise for the future, and, secondly, his refusal to receive the French Ambassador, with the communication of this refusal, as was alleged, "officially to the Cabinets of Europe" which was a mistaken allegation;

and the paper concludes by announcing that on the preceding day they had called out the reserves, and that they should immediately take the measures necessary to guard the interests, the security, and the honor of France. This was war.

Some there were who saw the fearful calamity, the ghastly crime, then and there initiated. The scene that ensued belongs to this painful record. The paper announcing war was followed by applause, with cries of "Bravo!" The Prime Minister added soon after in debate, that he accepted war with "a light heart." Not all were in this mood. Esquiros, the Republican, cried from his seat, in momentous words, "You have a light heart, and the blood of nations is about to flow!" To the apology of the Prime Minister, "that in the discharge of a duty the heart is not troubled," Jules Favre, the Republican leader, of acknowledged moderation and ability, flashed forth, "When the discharge of this duty involves the slaughter of two nations, we may well have the heart troubled!" Beyond these declarations, giving utterance to the natural sentiments of humanity, was the positive objection most forcibly presented by Thiers, so famous in the Chamber and in literature, that France had obtained a concession from Prussia, "which expiated by a check the grave fault it had committed,"—that France had prevailed in substance, and all that remained was "a question of form," "a question of words and susceptibilities," "questions of etiquette." The experienced statesman asked for the despatches. Then came a confession. The Prime Minister replied, that he had "nothing to communicate,—that, in the true sense of the term, there had been no despatches,—that there were only verbal communications preserved in reports, which, according to diplomatic usage, are not communicated." Here Emmanuel Arago interrupted: "It is on these reports that you make war!" The Prime Minister proceeded to read two brief telegrams from Count Benedetti at Ems, when De Choiseul very justly exclaimed: "We cannot make war on that ground; it is impossible!" Others cried out from their seats, — Garnier-Pagès saying, "These are phrases"; Emmanuel Arago protesting, "On this the civilized world will pronounce you wrong"; to which Jules Favre added, "Unhappily, true!" Thiers and Jules Favre, with vigorous eloquence, charged the war upon the Cabinet, — Thiers declaring, "I regret to be obliged to say that we have war by the fault of the Cabinet"; Jules Favre alleging, "If we have war, it is thanks to the politics of the Cabinet, — from the exposition made, so far as the general interests of the country are concerned, there is no avowable motive to war." Girault exclaimed, in similar spirit: "We would be among the first to come forward in a war for the country, but we do not wish to come forward in a dynastic and aggressive war." The Duc de Gramont, who on the 6th of July flung down the gauntlet, spoke once more for the Cabinet, stating solemnly, what was not the fact, that the Prussian Government had communicated to all the Cabinets of Europe the refusal to receive the French Ambassador, and then on this misstatement ejaculating: "It is an outrage on the Emperor and on France; and if by impossibility there should be in my country a Chamber that would hear and tolerate it, I would not remain five minutes Minister of Foreign Affairs." In our country we have seen how the Southern heart was fired; so also was fired the heart of France. The Duke descended from the tribune amidst prolonged applause, with cries of "Bravo!" followed at his seat, so says the report, by numerous felicitations. Such was the atmosphere of the Chamber at this eventful moment. The orators of the Opposition, pleading for delay in the interest of peace, were stifled, and when Gambetta, the young and fearless Republican, made himself heard in calling for the text of the despatch communicating the refusal to receive the Ambassador, to the end that the Chamber, France, and all Europe might judge of its character, he was answered by the Prime Minister with the taunt that "for the first time in a French Assembly there were such difficulties on a certain side, in explaining *a question of honor.*" Such was the case as presented by the Prime Minister, and on this question of honor he accepted war "with a light heart." Better say with no heart at all, — for whoso could find in this condition of things sufficient reason for war was without heart.

During these brief days of solicitude, from the 6th to the 15th of July, England made an unavailing effort for peace. Lord Lyons was indefatigable, and he was sustained at home by Lord Granville, who as a last resort reminded the two parties of the stipulation at the Congress of Paris, which they had accepted, in favor of Arbitration as a substitute for War, and asked them to accept the good offices of some friendly Power. This most reasonable proposition was rejected by the French Minister, who gave new point to the French case by charging that Prussia "had chosen to declare that France had been affronted in the person of her Ambassador," and then positively insisting that "it was this boast which was the *gravamen* of the offence." Capping the climax of barbarous absurdity, the French Minister did not hesitate to announce that this "constituted an insult which no nation of any spirit could brook, and rendered it, much to the regret of the French Government, impossible to take into consideration the mode of settling the original matter in dispute which was recommended by her Majesty's Government." (Lord Lyons to Lord Granville, July 16, 1870.) Thus was peaceful Arbitration repelled. All honor to the English Government for proposing it!

The famous telegram put forward by France as the *gravamen*, or chief offence, was not communicated to the Chamber. The Prime Minister, though hard pressed, held it back. Was it from conviction of its too trivial character? But it is not lost to the history of the duel. This telegram, with something of the brevity peculiar to telegraphic despatches, merely reports the refusal to see the French Ambassador, without one word of affront or boast. It reports the fact and nothing else, and it is understood that the refusal was only when this functionary presented himself the third time on the same business. Considering the interests involved, it would have been better, had the King seen him as many times as he chose to call; yet the refusal was not unnatural. The perfect courtesy of his Majesty on this occasion furnished no cause of complaint. All that remained for pretext was the telegram.

FORMAL DECLARATION OF WAR.

The scene in the Legislative Body was followed by the instant introduction of bills making additional appropriations for the Army and Navy, calling out the

National Guard, and authorizing volunteers for the war. This last proposition was commended by the observation that in France there was a quantity of young people liking powder, but not liking barracks, who would in this way be suited; and this was received with applause. On the 18th of July there was a further appropriation to the extent of 500 million francs, — 450 millions being for the Army and 50 for the Navy, — and from 150 to 500 millions treasury notes were authorized. On the 20th of July, the Duc de Gramont appeared once more at the tribune, and made the following speech: —

"Conformably to customary rules, and by order of the Emperor, I have invited the *Chargé d'Affaires* of France to notify the Berlin Cabinet of our resolution to seek by arms the guaranties which we have not been able to obtain by discussion. This step has been accomplished, and I have the honor of making known to the Legislative Assembly that in consequence a state of war exists between France and Prussia, beginning the 19th of July. This declaration applies equally to the allies of Prussia, who lend her the co-operation of their arms against us."

Here the French Minister played the part of trumpeter in the duel, making proclamation before his champion rode forward. According to the statement of Count Bismarck, made to the Parliament at Berlin, this formal Declaration of War was the solitary official communication from France in this whole transaction, being the first and only note since the candidature of Prince Leopold. How swift this madness will be seen in a few dates. On the 6th of July was uttered the first defiance from the French tribune; on the 15th of July an exposition of the griefs of France, in the nature of a

Declaration of War, with a demand for men and money; on the 19th of July a state of war was declared to exist. Firmly, but in becoming contrast with the "light heart" of France, this was promptly accepted by Germany, whose heart and strength found expression in the speech of the King at the opening of Parliament, hastily assembled on the 19th of July. With articulation disturbed by emotion and with moistened eyes, his Majesty said, "Leaning on the unanimous will of the German governments of the South, as of the governments of the North, we address ourselves to the patriotism and devotion of the German people for the defence of their honor and their independence." Parliament responded sympathetically to the King, and made the necessary appropriations. And thus the two champions stood front to front.

THE TWO HOSTILE PARTIES.

Throughout France, throughout Germany, the trumpet sounded, and everywhere the people sprang to arms, as if the great horn of Orlando, after a sleep of ages, had sent forth once more its commanding summons. Not a town, not a village, that the voice did not penetrate. Modern invention had supplied an ally beyond anything in fable. From all parts of France, from all parts of Germany, armed men leaped forward, leaving behind the charms of peace and the business of life. On each side the muster was mighty, armies counting by the hundred thousand. And now, before we witness the mutual slaughter, let us pause to consider the two parties, and the issue between them.

France and Germany are most unlike, and yet the peers of each other, while among the nations they are unsurpassed in civilization, each prodigious in resources, splendid in genius, and great in renown. No two nations are so nearly matched. By Germany now I mean not only the States constituting North Germany, but also Würtemberg, Baden, and Bavaria of South Germany, allies in the present war, all of which together make fifty-two millions of French hectares, being the exact area of France. The population of each is not far from thirty-eight millions, and it would be difficult to say which is the larger. Looking at finances, Germany has the smaller revenue, but also the smaller debt, while her rulers, following the sentiment of the people, cultivate a wise economy, so that here again substantial equality is maintained with France. The armies of the two, embracing regular troops and those subject to call, did not differ much in numbers, unless we set aside the authority of the Almanach de Gotha, which puts the military force of France somewhat vaguely at 1,350,000, while that of North Germany is only 977,262, to which must be added 60,000 for Bavaria, 35,000 for Würtemberg, and 43,000 for Baden, making a sum-total of 1,115,262. This, however, is chiefly on paper, where it is evident France is stronger than in reality. Her available force at the outbreak of the war probably did not amount to more than 350,000 bayonets, while that of Germany, owing to her superior system, was as much as double this number. In Prussia every man is obliged to serve, and, still further, every man is educated. Discipline and education are two potent adjuncts. This is favorable to Germany. In the chassepot and needle-gun the two are equal. But France excels in a well-appointed Navy, having no less than fifty-five iron-clads and numerous other vessels of war, while Germany has not a single iron-clad and very few war-ships of any kind. Then again for long generations has existed another disparity, to the great detriment of Germany. France has been a nation, while Germany was divided, and therefore weak. Strong in union, the latter now claims something more than that "dominion of the air" once acknowledged to be hers, while France had the land and England the sea. The dominion of the land is at last contested, and we are saddened inexpressibly, that, from the elevation they have reached, these two peers of civilization can descend to practise the barbarism of war, and especially that the land of Descartes, Pascal, Voltaire, and Laplace must challenge to bloody duel the land of Luther, Leibnitz, Kant, and Humboldt.

FOLLY.

Plainly between these two neighboring Powers there has been unhappy antagonism, constant, if not increasing, partly from the memory of other days, and partly because France could not bear to witness that German unity which was a national right and duty. Often it has been said that war was inevitable. But it has come at last by surprise, and on a "question of form." So it was called by Thiers; so it was recognized by Ollivier, when he complained of insensibility to a question of honor; and so also by the Duc de Gramont, when he referred it all to a telegram. This is not the first time in history that wars have been waged on trifles; but since the Lord of Prauenstein challenged the Free City of Frankfort because a young lady of the city refused to dance with his uncle, nothing has passed more absurd than this challenge sent by

France to Germany, because the King of Prussia refused to see the French Ambassador in a third visit on the same matter, and then let the refusal be reported by telegraph. Here is the folly exposed by Shakespeare, when Hamlet touches a madness greater than his own in that spirit which would "find quarrel in a straw when honor's at the stake," and at the same time depicts an army

> " Led by a delicate and tender prince,
> Exposing what is mortal and unsure
> To all that fortune, death, and danger dare,
> *Even for an eggshell.*"

There can be no quarrel in a straw or for an eggshell, unless men have gone mad. Nor can honor in a civilized age require any sacrifice of reason or humanity.

UNJUST PRETENSION OF FRANCE TO INTERFERE WITH THE CANDIDATURE OF HOHENZOLLERN.

If the utter triviality of the pretext were left doubtful in the debate, if its towering absurdity were not plainly apparent, if its simple wickedness did not already stand before us, we should find all these characteristics glaringly manifest in that unjust pretension which preceded the objection of form, on which France finally acted. A few words will make this plain.

In a happy moment Spain rose against Queen Isabella, and amidst cries of "Down with the Bourbons!" drove her from the throne which she dishonored. This was in September, 1868. Instead of constituting a Republic at once, in harmony with those popular rights which had been proclaimed, the half-hearted leaders proceeded to look about for a King, and from that time till now they have been in this quest, as if it were the Holy Grail, or happiness on earth. The Royal Family of Spain was declared incompetent. Therefore a king must be found outside, — and so the quest was continued in other lands. One day the throne is offered to a prince of Portugal, then to a prince of Italy, but declined by each, — how wisely the future will show. At last, after a protracted pursuit of nearly two years, the venturesome soldier who is captain-general and prime minister, Marshal Prim, conceives the idea of offering it to a prince of Germany. His luckless victim is Prince Leopold Hohenzollern-Sigmaringen, a Catholic, thirty-five years of age, and colonel of the first regiment of the Prussian foot-guards, whose father, a mediatized German prince, resides at Düsseldorf. The Prince had not the good sense to decline. How his acceptance excited the French Cabinet, and became the beginning of the French pretext, I have already exposed; and now I come to the pretension itself.

By what title did France undertake to interfere with the choice of Spain? If the latter was so foolish as to seek a foreigner for king, making a German first among Spaniards, by what title did any other Power attempt to control its will? To state the question is to answer it. Beginning with an outrage on Spanish independence, which the Spain of an earlier day would have resented, the next outrage was on Germany, in assuming that an insignificant prince of that country could not be permitted to accept the invitation, — all of which, besides being of insufferable insolence, was in that worst dynastic spirit which looks to princes rather than the people. Plainly France was unjustifiable. When I say it was none of her business, I give it the mildest condemnation. This was the first step in her monstrous *blunder-crime*.

Its character as a pretext becomes painfully manifest when we learn more of the famous Prince Leopold, thus invited by Spain and opposed by France. It is true that his family name is in part the same as that of the Prussian king. Each is Hohenzollern; but he adds Sigmaringen to the name. The two are different branches of the same family; but you must ascend to the twelfth century, and count more than thirty degrees, before you come to a common ancestor. And yet on this most distant and infinitesimal relationship the French pretension is founded. But audacity changes to the ridiculous when it is known that the Prince is nearer in relationship to the French Emperor than to the Prussian King, and this by three different intermarriages, which do not go back to the twelfth century. Here is the case. His grandfather had for wife the daughter of Joachim Murat, King of Naples, and brother-in-law of the first Napoleon; and his father had for wife the daughter of Stéphanie de Beauharnais, the adopted daughter of the first Napoleon; so that Prince Leopold is by his father great-grandson of Murat, and by his mother he is grandson of Stéphanie de Beauharnais, adopted daughter of the first Napoleon, and aunt to the present Emperor; and to this may be added still another connection, by the marriage of his father's sister with Joachim Napoleon, Marquis de Pepoli, grandson of Murat. It was natural that a person thus connected with the Imperial Family should be a welcome visitor at the Tuileries; and it is easy to believe that Marshal Prim, who offered him the throne, was encouraged to believe that the Emperor's kinsman and guest would be favorably regarded by France. And yet, in the face of these things, and the three several family ties, fresh and modern, binding him to France and the French Emperor, the pretension was set up that his occupation of the Spanish throne would put in peril the interests and the honor of France.

BECAUSE FRANCE WAS READY.

In sending defiance to Prussia on this question, the French Cabinet selected their own ground. Evidently a war had been meditated, and the candidature of Prince Leopold from beginning to end supplied a pretext. In this conclusion, which is too obvious, we are hardly left to inference. The secret was disclosed by Rouher, President of the Senate, lately the eloquent and unscrupulous Minister, when, in an official address to the Emperor, immediately after the War Manifesto read by the Prime Minister, he declared that France quivered with indignation at the excesses of an ambition over-excited by the one day's good fortune at Sadowa, and then proceeded: " Animated by the calm hope which is the true force of the Empire, your Majesty knew how to wait; but in the four last years you have perfected an armament of soldiers, and raised to the highest pitch the organization of our military forces. *Thanks to your care, Sire, France is ready.*" Thus, according to the President of the Senate, did France, after waiting, commence war because she was ready, while, according to the Cabinet, it was on the point of honor. Both were right. The war was declared because the Emperor thought himself ready, and a pretext was found in the affair of the telegram.

Considering the age, and the present demands of civilization, such a war stands forth terrific in wrong, making the soul rise indignant against it. One reason avowed is brutal; the other is frivolous; both are criminal. If we look into the text of the manifesto and the speeches of the Cabinet, it is a war founded on a trifle, on a straw, on an eggshell. Obviously these were pretexts only. Therefore it is a war of pretexts, the real object being the humiliation and dismemberment of Germany, in the vain hope of exalting the French Empire and perpetuating a bauble gimcrack crown on the head of a boy. By military success and a peace dictated at Berlin, the Emperor trusted to find himself in such condition that, on return to Paris, he could overthrow parliamentary government so far as it existed there, and re-establish personal government, where all depended upon himself, — thus making triumph over Germany the means of another triumph over the French people. In other times there have been wars as criminal in origin, where trifle, straw, or eggshell, played its part, but they contrasted less with the surrounding civilization. To this list belong the frequent Dynastic Wars, prompted by the interest, the passion, or the whim of some one in the Family of Kings. Others have begun in recklessness kindred to that we now witness, — as when England entered into war with Holland, and for reason did not hesitate to allege an offensive picture in the Town Hall of Amsterdam. The England of Charles II. was hardly less sensitive than the France of Louis Napoleon, while in each was similar indifference to consequences. But France has precedents of her own. From the remarkable correspondence of the Princess Palatine, Duchess of Orléans, we learn that one of the wars with Holland under Louis XIV. was brought on by the Minister, De Lyonne, that he might give employment out of France to a personage who had made him jealous of his wife. (*Lettre de* 31 *Mars,* 1715, Tome I. p. 389.) The communicative and exuberant Saint-Simon tells us twice over how Louvois, another Minister of Louis XIV., being overruled by his master with regard to the dimensions of a window at Versailles, was filled with the idea that "on account of a few inches in a window," as he expressed it, all his services would be forgotten, and therefore, to save his place, excited a foreign war that would make him necessary to the king. The flames in the Palatinate, devouring the works of man, attested his continuing power. (Saint-Simon, *Mémoires,* Tome VII. p. 49; XIII. p. 10.) The war became general, but, according to the chronicler, it ruined France at home, and did not extend it abroad. The French Emperor confidently expected to occupy the same historic region so often burnt and ravaged by French arms, with that castle of Heidelberg which repeats the tale of blood, and, let me say, on no better reason than his royal predecessor, stimulated by an unprincipled Minister, anxious for personal position. The parallel is continued in the curse which the Imperial arms have brought on France.

PROGRESS OF THE WAR.

How this war proceeded I need not recount. You have all read the record day by day, sorrowing for Humanity, — how, after briefest interval of preparation or hesitation, the two combatants first crossed swords at Saarbrücken, within the German frontier, and the young Prince Imperial performed his part in picking up a bullet from the field, which the Emperor promptly reported by telegraph to the Empress, — how this little military success is all that was vouchsafed to the man who began the war, — how on the 2d of August, fourteen days after the formal Declaration, the Germans first trod the soil of France, — how soon thereafter victory followed, first on the hillsides of Wissembourg and then of Woerth, shattering the army of McMahon, to which the Empire was looking so confidently, — how another large army under Bazaine was driven within the strong fortress of Metz, — how all the fortresses, bristling with guns and frowning upon Germany, were invested, — how battle followed battle on various fields, where Death was the great conqueror, — how, with help of modern art, war showed itself to be murder by machinery, — how McMahon, gathering together his scattered men and strengthening them with reinforcements, attempted to relieve Bazaine, — how at last, after long marches, his large army found itself shut up at Sedan with a tempest of fire beating upon its huddled ranks, so that its only safety was capitulation, — how with the capitulation of the army was the submission of the Emperor himself, who gave his sword to the King of Prussia and became prisoner of war, — and how, on the reception of this news at Paris, Louis Napoleon and his dynasty were divested of their powers and the Empire was lost in the Republic. These things you know. I need not dwell on them. Not to battles and their fearful vicissitudes, where all is incarnadined with blood, must we look, but to the ideas which prevail, — as for the measure of time we look, not to the pendulum in its oscillations, but to the clock in the tower, whose striking tells the hours. A great hour for Humanity sounded when the Republic was proclaimed. And this I say, even should it fail again ; for every attempt contributes to the final triumph.

A WAR OF SURPRISES.

The war, from the pretext at its beginning to the capitulation at Sedan, has been a succession of surprises, where the author of the pretext was a constant sufferer. Nor is this strange. Falstaff says, with humorous point, "See now how wit may be made a jack-a-lent, when 't is upon ill employment"; and another character, in a play of Beaumont and Fletcher, reveals the same evil destiny in stronger terms, when he says, —

"Hell gives us art to reach the depths of sin,
But leaves us wretched fools when we are in."

And this was precisely the condition of the French Empire. Germany perhaps had one surprise, at the sudden adoption of the pretext for war. But the Empire has known nothing but surprise. A fatal surprise was the promptitude with which all the German States, outside of Austrian rule, accepted the leadership of Prussia, and joined their forces to hers. Differences were forgotten, whether the hate of Hanover, the dread of Würtemberg, the coolness of Bavaria, the opposition of Saxony, or the impatience of the Hanse Towns at lost importance. Hanover would not rise; the other States and cities would not be detached. On the day after the reading of the War Manifesto at the French tribune, even before the King's speech to the Northern Parliament, the Southern States began to move. German unity stood firm, and this was the supreme surprise for France with which the war began. On one day the Emperor in his Official Journal declares his object to be the deliverance of Bavaria from Prussian oppression, and on the very next day the Crown Prince of

Prussia, at the head of Bavarian troops, crushes an Imperial army.

Then came the manifest inferiority of the Imperial army, everywhere outnumbered, which was another surprise, — the manifest inferiority of the Imperial artillery, also a surprise, — the manifest inferiority of the Imperial generals, still a surprise. Above these was a prevailing inefficiency and improvidence, which very soon became conspicuous, and this was a surprise. The strength of Germany, as now exhibited, was a surprise. And when the German armies entered France, every step was a surprise. Wissembourg was a surprise; so was Woerth; so was Beaumont; so was Sedan. Every encounter was a surprise. Abel Drout, the French general who fell bravely fighting at Wissembourg, the first sacrifice on the battle-field, was surprised; so was McMahon, not only at the beginning, but at the end. He thought that the King and Crown Prince were marching on Paris. So they were, — but they turned aside for a few days to surprise a whole army of more than a hundred thousand men, terrible with cannon and newly invented implements of war, under a Marshal of France, and with an Emperor besides. As this succession of surprises was crowned with what seemed the greatest surprise of all, there remained a greater still in the surprise of the French Empire. No Greek Nemesis with unrelenting hand ever dealt more incessantly the unavoidable blow, until the Empire fell as a dead body falls, while the Emperor became a captive and the Empress a fugitive, with their only child a fugitive also. The poet says: —

> "Sometime let gorgeous Tragedy
> In sceptred pall come sweeping by."

It has swept before the eyes of all. Beneath that sceptred pall is the dust of a great Empire, founded and ruled by Louis Napoleon; if not the dust of the Emperor also, it is because he was willing to sacrifice others rather than himself.

OTHER FRENCH SOVEREIGNS CAPTURED ON THE BATTLE-FIELD.

Twice before have French sovereigns yielded on the battle-field, and become prisoners of war; but never before was capitulation so vast. Do their fates furnish any lesson? At the Battle of Poictiers, memorable in English history, John, King of France, became the prisoner of Edward the Black Prince. His nobles, one after another, fell by his side, but he contended valiantly to the last, until, spent with fatigue and overcome by numbers, he surrendered. His son, of the same age as the son of the French Emperor, was wounded while battling for his father. The courtesy of the English Prince conquered more than his arms. I quote the language of Hume: "More touched by Edward's generosity than by his own calamities, he confessed that, notwithstanding his defeat and captivity, his honor was still unimpaired, and that, if he yielded the victory, it was at least gained by a prince of such consummate valor and humanity." (Hume's History of England, Chap. XVI.) The King was taken to England, where, after swelling the triumphal pageant of his conqueror, he made a disgraceful treaty for the dismemberment of France, which the indignant nation would not ratify. A captivity of more than four years was terminated by a ransom of three million crowns in gold,— an enormous sum, more than ten million dollars in our day. Evidently the King was unfortunate, for he did not continue in France, but, under the influence of motives differently stated, returned to England, where he died. Surely here is a lesson.

More famous than John was Francis, with salamander crest, also King of France, and rich in gayety, whose countenance, depicted by that art of which he was the patron, stands forth conspicuous in the line of kings. As the French Emperor attacked Germany, so did the King enter Italy, and he was equally confident of victory. On the field of Pavia he encountered an army of Charles V., but commanded by his generals, when, after fighting desperately and killing seven men with his own hand, he was compelled to surrender. His mother was at the time regent of France, and to her he is said to have written the sententious letter, " All is lost except honor." No such letter was written by Francis, nor do we know of any such letter by Louis Napoleon; but the situation of the two regents was identical. Here are the words in which Hume describes the condition of the earlier: " The princess was struck with the greatness of the calamity. She saw the kingdom without a sovereign, without an army, without generals, without money, surrounded on every side by implacable and victorious enemies, and her chief resource in her present distresses were the hopes she entertained of peace and even of assistance from the King of England." (Hume's History, Chap. XXIX.) Francis became the prisoner of Charles V., and was conveyed to Madrid, where, after a year of captivity, he was at length released, when, crossing the French frontier, he galloped forward, crying out, " I am yet a king!" Is not the fate of Louis Napoleon prefigured in the exile and death of his royal predecessor John, rather than in the return of Francis with his delighted cry?

LOUIS NAPOLEON.

The fall of Louis Napoleon is natural. It is hard to see how it could be otherwise, so long as we continue

> "to assert eternal Providence,
> And justify the ways of God to man."

Had he remained successful to the end, and died peacefully on the throne, his name would have been a perpetual encouragement to dishonesty and crime. By treachery without parallel, breaking repeated promises and his oath of office, he was able to trample on the Republic. Taking his place in the National Assembly after long exile, the adventurer made haste to declare exultation in regaining his country and all his rights as citizen, with the ejaculation, "The Republic has done me this good! let the Republic receive my oath of gratitude, my oath of devotion!" and next he proclaimed that there was nobody to surpass him in determined consecration "to the defence of order and to the establishment of the Republic." Good words these. Then again, when candidate for the Presidency, in a manifesto to the electors he gave another pledge, announcing that he "would devote himself altogether, without mental reservation, to the establishment of a Republic, wise in its laws, honest in its counsels, great and strong in its acts," and he volunteered further words, binding him in special loyalty, saying that he "should make it a *point of honor* to leave to his successor, at the end of four years, power strengthened, liberty intact, real progress accomplished." How these plain and unequivocal engagements were openly broken you shall see.

Chosen by the popular voice, his inauguration took place as President of the Republic, when he solemnly renewed the engagements already assumed. Ascending from his seat in the Assembly to the tribune, and holding up his hand, he took the following oath of office: "In presence of God, and before the French people, represented by the National Assembly, I swear to continue faithful to the Democratic Republic one and indivisible, and to perform all the duties which the Constitution imposes upon me." This was an oath. Then, addressing the Assembly, he said: "The suffrages of the nation and the oath which I have just taken prescribe my future conduct. My duty is traced. I will perform it as *a man of honor.*" Again he attests his honor. Then, after deserved tribute to his immediate predecessor and rival, General Cavaignac, on his loyalty of character, and that sentiment of duty which he declares to be "the first quality in the chief of a State," he renews his vows to the Republic, saying, "We have, citizen representatives, a great mission to fulfil; it is to found a Republic in the interest of all"; and he closed amidst cheers for the Republic. And yet, in the face of this oath of office and this succession of most solemn pledges, where he twice attests his honor, he has hardly become President before he commences plotting to make himself Emperor, until at last, by violence and blood, with brutal butchery in the streets of Paris, he succeeded in overthrowing the Republic, to which he was bound by obligations of gratitude and duty, as well as by engagements in such various form. The Empire was declared. Then followed his marriage, and a dynastic ambition to assure the crown for his son.

Early in life a "charcoal" conspirator against kings, he now became a crowned conspirator against republics. The name of Republic was to him a reproof, while its glory was a menace. Against the Roman Republic he conspired early; and when the Rebellion waged by Slavery seemed to afford opportunity, he conspired against our Republic, promoting as far as he dared the independence of the Slave States, and at the same time on the ruins of the Mexican Republic setting up a mock Empire. In similar spirit has he conspired against German unity, whose just strength promised to be a wall against his unprincipled self-seeking.

This is but an outline of that incomparable perfidy, which, after a career of seeming success, is brought to a close. Of a fallen man I would say nothing; but, for the sake of humanity, Louis Napoleon should be exposed. He was of evil example, extending with his influence. To measure the vastness of this detriment is impossible. In sacrificing the Republic to his own aggrandizement, in ruling for a dynasty rather than the people, in subordinating the peace of the world to his own wicked ambition for his boy, he set an example of selfishness, and in proportion to his triumph was mankind corrupted in its judgment of human conduct. Teaching men to seek ascendency at the expense of duty, he demoralized not only France, but the world. Unquestionably part of this evil example was his falsehood to the Republic. Promise, pledge, honor, oath, were all violated in this monstrous treason. Never in history was greater turpitude. Unquestionably he could have saved the Republic, but he preferred his own exaltation. As I am a Republican, and believe republican institutions for the good of mankind, I cannot pardon the traitor. The people of France are ignorant; he did not care to have them educated, for their ignorance was his strength. With education bestowed, the Republic would have been assured. And even after the Empire, had he thought more of education and less of his dynasty, there would have been a civilization throughout France making war impossible. Unquestionably the present war is his work, instituted for his imagined advantage. Bacon, in one of his remarkable apothegms, tells us that "Extreme self-lovers will set a man's house on fire, though it were but to roast their eggs." Louis Napoleon has set Europe on fire to roast his.

Beyond the continuing offence of his public life, I charge upon him three special and unpardonable crimes: first, that violation of public duty and public faith, contrary to all solemnities of promise, by which the whole order of society was weakened and human character was degraded; secondly, disloyalty to republican institutions, so that through him the Republic has been arrested in Europe; and, thirdly, this cruel and causeless war of which he is the guilty author.

RETRIBUTION.

Of familiar texts in Scripture, there is one which, since the murderous outbreak, has been of constant applicability and force. You know it: "All they that take the sword shall perish with the sword": and these words are addressed to nations as to individuals. France took the sword against Germany, and now lies bleeding at every pore. Louis Napoleon took the sword, and is naught. Already in that *coup d'état* by which he overthrew the Republic he took the sword, and now the Empire, which was the work of his hands, expires. In Mexico again he took the sword, and again paid the fearful penalty, while the Austrian Archduke, who, yielding to his pressure, made himself Emperor there, was shot by order of the Mexican President, an Indian of unmixed blood. And here there was retribution, not only for the French Emperor, but far beyond. I know not if there be invisible threads by which the present is attached to the distant past, making the descendant suffer even for a distant ancestor, but I cannot forget that Maximilian was derived from that very family of Charles V. whose conquering general, Cortés, stretched the Indian Guatimozin upon a bed of fire, and afterwards executed him on a tree. The death of Maximilian was tardy retribution for the death of Guatimozin. And thus in this world is wrong avenged, sometimes after many generations. The fall of the French Emperor is an illustration of that same retribution which is so constant. While he yet lives, judgment has begun.

If I accumulate instances, it is because the certainty of retribution for wrong, and especially for the great wrong of war, is a lesson of the present duel to be impressed. Take notice, all who would appeal to war, that the way of the transgressor is hard, and sooner or later he is overtaken. The ban may fall tardily, but it is sure to fall.

Retribution in another form has already visited France; nor is its terrible vengeance yet spent. Not only are populous cities, all throbbing with life and filled with innocent households, subjected to siege, but to bombardment also, being that most ruthless trial of war, where non-combatants, including women and children, sick and aged, share with the soldier his peculiar perils, and suffer alike with him. All are equal before the hideous shell, crashing, bursting, destroying, killing, and changing the fairest scene into blood-spattered wreck. Against its vengeful, slaughterous descent there is no protection for the people, nothing but an uncertain shelter in cellars, or, it may be, in the common sewers. Already Strasbourg, Toul, and Metz have been called to endure this indiscriminate massacre, where there is no distinction of persons; and now the same fate is threatened to Paris the beautiful, with its thronging population counted by the million. Thus is the ancient chalice which France handed to others now commended to her own lips. It was France that first in history adopted this method of war. Long ago, under Louis XIV., it became a favorite; but it has not escaped the judgment of history. Voltaire, with elegant pen, records that "this art, carried soon among other nations, served only to multiply human calamities, and more than once was dreadful to France, where it was invented." (Voltaire, *Siècle de Louis XIV.*, Chap. XIV.) The bombardment of Luxemburg in 1683 drew from Sismondi, always humane and refined, words applicable to recent events. "Louis XIV.," he says, "was the first to put in practice the atrocious method, newly invented, of bombarding towns, ... of attacking, not fortifications, but private houses, not soldiers, but peaceable inhabitants, women and children, and of confounding thousands of private crimes, each one of which would cause horror, in one great public crime, one great disaster, which he regarded only as one of the catastrophes of war." (Sismondi, *Histoire des Français,* Tome XXV. p. 452.) Again is the saying fulfilled, "All they that take the sword shall perish with the sword." No lapse of time can avert the inexorable law. Macbeth saw it in his terrible imaginings when he said, —

> " But in these cases
> We still have judgment here; that we but teach
> Bloody instructions, which, being taught, return
> To plague the inventor."

And what instruction more bloody than the bombardment of a city, which now returns to plague the French people?

Thus is history something more even than philosophy teaching by example; it is sermon with argument and exhortation. The simple record of nations preaches; and whether you regard reason or the affections, it is the same. If nations were wise or humane, they would not fight.

PEACE AFTER CAPITULATION AT SEDAN.

Vain are lessons of the past or texts of prudence against that spirit of War which finds sanction and regulation in International Law. So long as the war system continues, men will fight. While I speak, the two champions still stand front to front, Germany exulting in victory, but France in no respect submissive. The duel still rages, although one of the champions is pressed to earth, as in that early combat where the Chevalier Bayard, so eminent in chivalry, thrust his dagger into the nostrils of his fallen foe, and then dragged his dead body off the field. History now repeats itself, and we witness in Germany the very conduct condemned in the famous French knight.

The French Emperor was the aggressor. He began this fatal duel. Let him fall, — but not the people of France. Cruelly already have they expiated their offence in accepting such a ruler. Not always should they suffer. Enough of waste, enough of sacrifice, enough of slaughter have they undergone. Enough have they felt the accursed hoof of war.

It is easy to see now, that, after the capitulation at Sedan, there was a double mistake: first, on the part of Germany, which, as magnanimous conqueror, should have proposed peace, thus conquering in character as in arms; and, secondly, on the part of the Republic, which should have declined to wage a war of Imperialism against which the Republican leaders had so earnestly protested. With the capitulation of the Emperor the dynastic question was closed. There was no longer pretension or pretext, nor was there occasion for war. The two parties should have come to an understanding. Why continue this terrible homicidal, fratricidal, suicidal combat, fraught with mutual death and sacrifice? Why march on Paris? Why beleaguer Paris? Why bombard Paris? To what end? If for the humiliation of France, then must it be condemned.

THREE ESSENTIAL CONDITIONS OF PEACE.

In arriving at terms of peace, there are at least three conditions which cannot be overlooked in the interest of civilization, and that the peace may be such in reality as in name, and not an armistice only, — three postulates which stand above all question, and dominate this debate, so that any essential departure from them must end in wretched failure.

The first is the natural requirement of Germany, that there shall be completest guaranty against future aggression, constituting what is so well known among us as "Security for the Future." Count Bismarck, with an exaggeration hardly pardonable, alleges more than twenty invasions of Germany by France, and declares that these must be stopped forever. Many or few, they must be stopped forever. The second condition to be regarded is the natural requirement of France, that the guaranty, while sufficient, shall be such as not to wound needlessly the sentiments of the French people, or to offend any principle of public law. It is difficult to question these two postulates, at least in the abstract. Only when we come to the application is there opportunity for difference. The third postulate, demanded alike by justice and humanity, is the establishment of some rule or precedent by which the recurrence of such a barbarous duel shall be prevented. It will not be enough to obtain a guaranty for Germany; there must be a guaranty for civilization itself.

On careful inquiry, it will be seen that all these can be accomplished in one way only, which I will describe, when I have first shown what is now put forward and discussed as the claim of Germany, under two different heads, indemnity and guaranty.

INDEMNITY OF GERMANY.

I have already spoken of guaranty as an essential condition. Indemnity is not essential. At the close of our war with Slavery we said nothing of indemnity. For the life of the citizen there could be no indemnity; nor was it practicable even for the treasure sacrificed.

Security for the Future was all that our nation required, and this was found in provisions of law and constitution establishing equal rights. From various intimations it is evident that Germany will not be content without indemnity in money on a large scale; and it is also evident that France, the aggressor, cannot, when conquered, deny liability to a certain extent. The question will be on the amount. Already German calculators begin to array their unrelenting figures. One of these insists that the indemnity shall not only cover outlay for the German army, — pensions of widows and invalids, — maintenance and support of French wounded and prisoners, — compensation to Germans expelled from France, — also damage suffered by the territory to be annexed, especially Strasbourg; but it is also to cover indirect damages, large in amount, — as, loss to the nation from change of productive laborers into soldiers, — loss from killing and disabling so many laborers, — and, generally, loss from suspension of trade and manufactures, depreciation of national property, and diminution of the public revenues, — all of which, according to a recent estimate, reach the fearful sum-total of 4,935,000,000 francs or nearly one thousand million dollars. Of this sum, 1,255,000,000 francs are on account of the army, 1,230,000,000 for direct damage, 2,250,000,000 for indirect damage, and 200,000,000 for damage to the reconquered provinces. Still further, the Berlin Chamber of Commerce insists on indemnity not only for actual loss of ships and cargoes from the blockade, but also for damages on account of detention. Much of this many-headed account, which I introduce in order to open the case in its extent, will be opposed by France, as fabulous, consequential, and remote. The practical question will be, Can one nation do wrong to another without paying for the damage, whatever it may be, direct or indirect, — always provided it be susceptible of estimate? Here I content myself with the remark, that, while, in the settlement of international differences, there is no place for technicality, there is always room for moderation.

GUARANTY OF DISMEMBERMENT.

Vast as may be the claim of indemnity, it opens no question so calculated to touch the sensibilities of France as the claim of guaranty already announced by Germany. On this head we are not left to conjecture. From her first victory we have been assured that Germany would claim Alsace and German Lorraine, with their famous strongholds; and now we have the statement of Count Bismarck, in a diplomatic circular, that he expects to remove the German frontier further west, meaning to the Vosges Mountains, if not to the Moselle also, and to convert the fortresses into what he calls "defensive strongholds of Germany." Then, with larger view, he declares, that, "in rendering it more difficult for France, from whom all European troubles have so long proceeded, to assume the offensive, we likewise promote the common interest of Europe, which demands the preservation of peace." Here is just recognition of peace as the common interest of Europe, to be assured by disabling France. How shall this be done? The German Minister sees nothing but dismemberment, consecrated by a Treaty of Peace. With diplomatic shears he would cut off a portion of French territory, and, taking from it the name of France, stamp upon it the trade-mark of

Germany. Two of its richest and most precious provinces, for two centuries constituent parts of the great nation, with that ancient cathedral city, the pride of the Rhine, long years ago fortified by Vauban as "the strongest barrier of France," are to be severed, and with them a large and industrious population, which, while preserving the German language, have so far blended with France as to become Frenchmen. This is the German proposition, which I call the guaranty of Dismemberment.

One argument for this proposition is brushed aside easily. Had the fortune of war been adverse to Germany, it is said, peace would have been dictated at Berlin, perhaps at Königsberg, and France would have carried her frontier eastward to the Rhine, dismembering Germany. Such, I doubt not, would have been the attempt. The conception is entirely worthy of that Imperial levity with which the war began. But the madcap menace of the French Empire cannot be the measure of German justice. It is for Germany to show, that, notwithstanding this wildness, she knows how to be just. Dismemberment on this account would be only another form of retaliation; but retaliation is barbarous.

To the argument, that these provinces, with their strongholds, are needed for the defence of Germany, there is the obvious reply, that, if cut off from France contrary to the wishes of the local population, and with the French people in chronic irritation on this account, they will be places of weakness rather than strength, strongholds of disaffection rather than defence, to be held always at the cannon's mouth. Does Germany seek lasting peace? Not in this way can it be had. A painful exaction, enforced by triumphant arms, must create a sentiment of hostility in France, suppressed for a season, but ready at a propitious moment to break forth in violence, so that between the two conterminous nations there will be nothing better than a peace where each sleeps on its arms, — which is but an Armed Peace. Such for weary years has been the condition of nations. Is Germany determined to prolong the awful curse? Will her most enlightened people, with poetry, music, literature, philosophy, science, and religion as constant ministers, to whom has been opened in rarest degree the whole book of knowledge, persevere in a brutal policy belonging to another age, and utterly alien to that superior civilization which is so truly theirs?

There is another consideration, not only of justice, but of public law, which cannot be overcome. The people of these provinces are unwilling to be separated from France. This is enough. France cannot sell or transfer them against their consent. Consult the great masters, and you will find their concurring authority. Grotius, from whom on such a question there can be no appeal, adjudges: "In the alienation of part of the sovereignty it is required *that the part to be alienated consent to the act.*" According to him, it must not be supposed "that the body should have the right of cutting off parts from itself and giving them into the authority of another." (Grotius, *De Jure Belli ac Pacis*, Lib. II. Cap. VI. § 4.) Of the same opinion is Puffendorff, declaring: "The sovereign who attempts to transfer his kingdom to another by his sole authority does an act in itself null and void, and not binding on his subjects. To make such a conveyance valid, the consent of the people is required, as well as of the Prince. (Puffendorff, Law of Nature and Nations, Book VIII. Chap. 5,

§ 9.) Vattel crowns this testimony, when he adds, that a province "abandoned and dismembered is not obliged to receive the new master attempted to be given it." (Vattel, Book II. Chap. 3, § 264.) Before such texts, stronger than a fortress, the soldiers of Germany must halt.

Nor can it be forgotten how inconsistent is the guaranty of Dismemberment with that heroic passion for national unity which is the glory of Germany. National unity is not less the right of France than of Germany; and these provinces, though in former centuries German, and still preserving the German speech, belong to the existing unity of France, — unless, according to the popular song, the German's Fatherland extends

"Far as the German accent rings";

and then the conqueror must insist on Switzerland; and why not cross the Atlantic, to dictate laws in Pennsylvania and Chicago? But this same song has a better verse, calling that the German's Fatherland

"Where in the heart love warmly lies."

But in these coveted provinces it is the love for France, and not for Germany, which prevails.

GUARANTY OF DISARMAMENT.

The guaranty of Dismemberment, when brought to the touchstone of the three essential conditions, is found wanting. Dismissing it as unsatisfactory, I come to that other guaranty where these conditions are all fulfilled, and we find security for Germany without offence to the just sentiments of France, and also a new safeguard to civilization. Against the guaranty of Dismemberment I oppose the guaranty of Disarmament. By

Disarmament I mean the razing of the French fortifications and the abolition of the standing army, except that minimum of force required for purposes of police. How completely this satisfies the conditions already named is obvious. For Germany there would be on the side of France absolute repose, so that Count Bismarck need not fear another invasion, — while France, saved from intolerable humiliation, would herself be free to profit by the new civilization.

Nor is this guaranty otherwise than practical in every respect, and the more it is examined will its inestimable advantage be apparent.

1. There is, first, its most obvious *economy*, which is so glaring that, according to a familiar French expression, "it leaps into the eyes." Undertaking even briefly to set it forth, I seem to follow the proverb and "show the sun with a lantern." According to the Almanach de Gotha, the appropriations for the army of France, during the year of peace before the war, were 588,852,970 francs, — or about one hundred and seventeen millions of dollars. Give up the Standing Army and this considerable sum disappears from the annual budget. But this retrenchment represents only partially the prodigious economy. Beyond the annual outlay is the loss to the nation by the change of producers into non-producers. Admitting that in France the average annual production of a soldier usefully employed would be only fifty dollars, and multiplying this small allowance by the numbers of the Standing Army, you have another amount to be piled upon the military appropriations. Is it too much to expect that this surpassing waste shall be stopped? Must the extravagance born of war, and nursed by long tradition, continue to drain the resources

of the land? Where is reason? Where humanity? A decree abolishing the Standing Army would be better for the French people, and more productive, than the richest gold-mine discovered in every department of France. Nor can imagination picture the fruitful result. I speak now only in the light of economy. Relieved from intolerable burden, industry would lift itself to unimagined labors, and society be quickened anew.

2. Beyond this economy, which need not be argued, is the positive *advantage, if not necessity*, of such change for France. I do not speak on general grounds applicable to all nations, but on grounds peculiar to France at the present moment. Emerging from a most destructive war, she will be subjected to enormous and unprecedented contributions of every kind. After satisfying Germany, she will find other obligations at home, — some pressing directly upon the nation, and others upon individuals. Beyond the outstanding pay of soldiers, requisitions for supplies, pensions for the wounded and the families of the dead, and other extraordinary liabilities accumulating as never before in the same time, there will be the duty of renewing that internal prosperity which has received such a shock; and here the work of restoration will be costly, whether to the nation or the individual. Revenue must be regained; roads and bridges repaired; markets supplied; nor can we omit the large and multitudinous losses from ravage of fields, seizure of stock, suspension of business, stoppage of manufactures, interference with agriculture, and the whole terrible drain of war by which the people are impoverished and disabled. If to the necessary appropriation and expenditure for all these things is superadded the annual tax of a Standing Army, and that

other draft from the change of producers into non-producers, plainly here is a supplementary burden of crushing weight. Talk of the last feather breaking the back of the camel, — but never was camel loaded down as France.

3. Beyond even these considerations of economy and advantage I put the transcendent, priceless benefit of Disarmament in the *assurance of peace*. Disarmament substitutes the constable for the soldier, and reduces the Standing Army to a police. The argument assumes, first, the needlessness of a Standing Army, and, secondly, its evil influence. Both of these points were touched at an early day by the wise Chancellor of England, Sir Thomas More, when, in his practical and personal Introduction to " Utopia " he alludes to what he calls the " bad custom" of keeping many servants, and then says: " In France there is yet a more pestiferous sort of people; for the whole country is full of soldiers, still kept up in time of peace, — if such a state of a nation may be called a peace." Then, proceeding with his judgment, the Chancellor holds up what he calls those " pretended statesmen " whose maxim is that it " is necessary for the public safety to have a good body of veteran soldiers ever in readiness." And after saying that these pretended statesmen " sometimes seek occasions for making war, that they may train up their soldiers in the art of cutting throats," he adds, in words soon to be tested, " But France has learned to its cost how dangerous it is to feed such beasts." It will be well, if France has learned this important lesson. The time has come to practise it.

All history is a vain word, and all experience is at fault, if large War Preparations, of which the Standing Army is the type, have not been constant provocatives of war. Pretended protectors against war, they have been real instigators to war. They have excited the evil against which they were to guard. The habit of wearing arms in private life exercised a kindred influence. So long as this habit continued society was darkened by personal combat, street-fight, duel, and assassination. The Standing Army is to the nation what the sword was to the modern gentleman, the stiletto to the Italian, the knife to the Spaniard, the pistol to our slave-master, — furnishing, like these, the means of death; and its possessor is not slow to use it. In stating the operation of this system, we are not left to inference. As France, according to Sir Thomas More, shows "how dangerous it is to feed such beasts," so does Prussia, in ever-memorable instance, which speaks now with more than ordinary authority, show precisely how the Standing Army may become the incentive to war. Frederick, the warrior king, is our witness. With honesty or impudence beyond parallel, he did not hesitate to record in his Memoirs, among the reasons for his war upon Maria Theresa, that, on coming to the throne, he found himself with "troops always ready to act." Voltaire, when called to revise the royal memoirs, erased this confession, but preserved a copy, so that by his literary activity we have this kingly authority for the mischief from a Standing Army. How complete a weapon was that army may be learned from Lafayette, who, in a letter to Washington, in 1786, after a visit to the King, described it thus: "Nothing can be compared to the beauty of the troops, to the discipline which reigns in all their ranks, to the simplicity of their movements, to the uniformity of their regiments. All the situations which can be supposed in war, all the movements which these must necessitate, have been by constant habit so inculcated in their heads, that all these operations are done almost mechanically." (Lafayette, *Mémoires*, Tome II. p. 133.) Nothing better has been devised since the Macedonian phalanx or the Roman legion. With such a weapon ready to his hands, the King struck Maria Theresa. And think you that the present duel between France and Germany could have been waged had not both nations found themselves, like Frederick of Prussia, "with troops always ready to act"? It was the possession of these troops which made the two parties rush so swiftly to the combat. Is not the lesson perfect? Already individuals have disarmed. Civilization requires that nations shall do likewise.

Thus is Disarmament enforced on three several grounds: first, economy; secondly, positive advantage, if not necessity, for France; and, thirdly, assurance of peace. No other guaranty promises so much. Does any other guaranty promise anything beyond the accident of force? Nor would France be alone. Dismissing to the arts of peace the large army victorious over Slavery, our Republic has shown how disarmament can be accomplished. The example of France, so entirely reasonable, so profitable, so pacific, and so harmonious with ours, would spread. Conquering Germany could not resist its influence. Nations are taught by example more than by precept, and either is better than force. Other nations would follow; nor would Russia, elevated by her great act of enfranchisement, fail to seize her sublime opportunity. Popular rights, which are strongest always in assured peace, would have new triumphs. Instead of Trial by Battle for the decision of differences between nations, there would be peaceful substitutes, as

Arbitration, or, it may be, a Congress of Nations, and the United States of Europe would appear above the subsiding waters. The old juggle of Balance of Power, which has rested like a nightmare on Europe, would disappear, like that other less bloody fiction of Balance of Trade, and nations, like individuals, would all be equal before the law. Here our own country furnishes an illustration. So long as Slavery prevailed among us there was an attempt to preserve what was designated balance of power between the North and South, pivoting on Slavery, — just as in Europe there has been an attempt to preserve balance of power among nations pivoting on War. Too tardily is it seen that this famous balance, which has played such a part at home and abroad, is but an artificial contrivance instituted by power, which must give place to a simple accord derived from the natural condition of things. Why should not the harmony which has begun at home be extended abroad? Practicable and beneficent here, it must be the same there. Then would nations exist without perpetual and reciprocal watchfulness. But the first step is to discard the wasteful, oppressive, and pernicious provocative to war, which is yet maintained at such terrible cost. To-day this glorious advance is presented to France and Germany.

KING WILLIAM AND COUNT BISMARCK.

Two personages at this moment hold in their hands the great question teeming with a new civilization. Honest and determined, both are patriotic rather than cosmopolitan or Christian, believing in Prussia rather than Humanity. And the patriotism so strong in each keeps still the early tinge of iron. I refer to King William and his Prime Minister, Count Bismarck.

More than any other European sovereign, William of Prussia possesses the infatuation of "divine right." He believes that he was appointed by God to be King, — differing here from Louis Napoleon, who in a spirit of compromise entitled himself Emperor " by the grace of God and the national will." This infatuation was illustrated at his coronation in ancient Königsberg, first home of Prussian royalty, and better famous as birthplace and lifelong home of Emmanuel Kant, when the King enacted a scene of melodrama which might be transferred from the church to the theatre. No other person was allowed to place the crown on his royal head. Lifting it from the altar, where it rested, he placed it there himself, in sign that he held it from Heaven and not from man, and next placed another on the head of the Queen, in sign that her dignity was derived from him. Then, turning round, he brandished a gigantic sword in testimony of readiness to defend the nation. Since the Battle of Sadowa, when the Austrian Empire was so suddenly shattered, he has believed himself providential sword-bearer of Germany, destined, perhaps, to revive the old glories of Barbarossa. His habits are soldierly, and, notwithstanding his seventy-three winters, he continues to find pleasure in wearing the spiked helmet of the Prussian camp. Republicans smile when he speaks of " my army," " my allies," and " my people "; but this egotism is the natural expression of the monarchical character, especially where the monarch believes that he holds by " divine right." His public conduct is in harmony with these conditions. He is a Protestant, and rules the land of

Luther, but he is no friend to modern Reform. The venerable system of war and prerogative is part of his inheritance handed down from fighting despots, and he evidently believes in it.

His Minister, Count Bismarck, is the partisan of "divine right," and, like the King, regards with satisfaction that hierarchical feudalism from which they are both derived. He is noble and believes in nobility. He believes also in force, as if he had the blood of the god Thor. He believes in war, and does not hesitate to throw its "iron dice," insisting upon the rigors of the game. As the German question began to lower, his policy was most persistent. "Not through speeches and votes of the majority," he said, in 1862, "are the great questions of the time decided, — that was the blunder of 1848 and 1849, — *but by steel and blood.*" Thus explicit was he. Having a policy, he became its representative, and very soon thereafter controlled the counsels of his sovereign, coming swiftly before the world; and yet his elevation was tardy. Born in 1815, he did not enter upon diplomacy until 1851, when thirty-six years of age, and only in 1862 became Prussian Minister at Paris, whence he was soon transferred to the Cabinet at Berlin as Prime Minister. Down to that time he was little known. His name is not found in any edition of the bulky French Dictionary of Contemporaries (Vapereau, *Dictionnaire des Contemporains*), not even its "additions and rectifications," until the Supplement of 1863. But from this time he drew so large a share of public attention that the contemporary press of the world became the dictionary where his name was always found. Nobody doubts his intellectual resources, his courage or strength of will, but it is felt that he is naturally hard, and little affected by human sympathy. Therefore is he an excellent war minister. It remains to be seen if he will do as much for peace. His one idea has been the unity of Germany under the primacy of Prussia, and here he encountered Austria, as he now encounters France. But in that larger unity, where nations will be conjoined in harmony, he can do less, so long at least as he continues a fanatic for kings and a cynic towards popular institutions.

Such is the King and such his Minister. I have described them that you may see how little help the great ideas already germinating from bloody fields will receive from them. In this respect they are as one.

TWO INFLUENCES VERSUS WAR SYSTEM.

Beyond the most persuasive influence of civilization, pleading as never before, with voice of reason and affection, that the universal tyrant and master-evil of Christendom, the War System, may cease, and the means now absorbed in its support be employed for the benefit of the Human Family, there are two special influences which cannot be without weight at this time. The first is German authority in the writings of philosophers, by whom Germany rules in thought; and the second is the uprising of the Working-Men: both against war as acknowledged arbiter between nations, and insisting upon peaceful substitutes.

AUTHORITY OF GERMAN MIND.

More than any other nation Germany has suffered from war. Without that fatal gift of beauty, " a dowry fraught with never-ending pains," which tempted the foreigner to Italy, her lot has been hardly less wretched; but Germany has differed from Italy in the successful bravery with which she repelled the invader. Tacitus says of her people, that, "girdled by many and most powerful tribes, they have been safe, not by submission, but by battles and perils";[1] and this same character, thus epigrammatically presented, has continued ever since. Yet this was not without that painful experience which teaches what art has so often attempted to picture and eloquence to describe, "The Miseries of War." Again in that same fearless spirit has Germany driven back the invader, while war is seen anew in its atrocious works. But it was not merely the "Miseries of War" which Germans regarded. The German mind is philosophical and scientific, and it early saw the irrational character of the War System. It is well known that Henry IV. of France conceived the idea of Harmony among nations without War, and his plan was taken up and elaborated in numerous writings by the good Abbé de Saint-Pierre, so that he made it his own. Rousseau in his treatise on the subject popularized Saint-Pierre. But it is to Germany that we must look for the most complete and practical development of this beautiful idea. If French in origin, it is German now in authority.

The greatest minds in Germany have dealt with this problem, and given to its solution the exactness of science. No greater have been applied to any question. Foremost in this list, in time and in fame, is Leibnitz, that marvel of human intelligence, second, perhaps, to

[1] "Plurimis ac valentissimis nationibus cincti, non per obsequium, sed prœliis et periclitando tuti sunt." — *De Moribus Germ.*, cap. 4.

none in history, who, on reading the Project for Perpetual Peace by the Abbé de Saint-Pierre, pronounced this judgment: "I have read it with attention, and am persuaded that such a Project is on the whole feasible, and that its execution would be one of the most useful things in the world." (Leibnitz, *Opera,* Vol. V. pp. 56 – 62, edit. Dutens.) Thus did Leibnitz affirm its feasibility and its immense usefulness. Other minds followed, in no apparent concert, but in unison. I may be pardoned, if, without being too bibliographical, I name some of these witnesses.

At Göttingen, renowned for its University, the question was opened, at the close of the Seven Years' War in 1763, in a work by Totze, whose character appears in its title, "Permanent and Universal Peace, according to the Plan of Henry IV." (*Ewiger und allgemeiner Friede nach der Entwurf Heinrichs IV.*) At Leipzig, also the seat of a University, the subject was presented in 1767 by Lilienfeld, in a treatise of much completeness, under the name of "New Constitution for States" (*Neues Staatsgebäude*), where, after exposing the wretched chances of the battle-field and the expense of armaments in time of peace, the author urges submission to Arbitrators, unless a Supreme Tribunal is established to administer International Law and to judge between nations. In 1804 appeared another work, of singular clearness and force, by Karl Schwab, entitled "Of Unavoidable Injustice" (*Ueber das unvermeidliche Unrecht*), where the author describes what he calls the Universal State, in which nations will be to each other as citizens in the Municipal State. He is not so visionary as to imagine that justice will always be inviolate between nations in the Universal State, for it is not always so between citizens in the Municipal State; but he confidently looks to the establishment between nations of the rules which now subsist between citizens, whose differences are settled peaceably by judicial tribunals.

These works, justly important for the light they shed, and as expressions of a growing sentiment, are eclipsed in the contributions of the great teacher, Emmanuel Kant, who, after his fame in philosophy was established, so that his works were discussed and expounded not only throughout Germany, but in other lands, in 1796 gave to the world a treatise entitled "On Perpetual Peace" (*Zum ewigen Frieden*), which was promptly translated into French, Danish, and Dutch. Two other works by him attest his interest in the subject, the first entitled "Idea for a General History in a Cosmopolitan View" (*Idee zu einer allgemeinen Geschichte in weltbürgerlicher Absicht*), and the other, "Metaphysical Elements of Jurisprudence" (*Metaphysische Anfangsgründe der Rechtslehre*). His grasp was complete. A treaty of peace which tacitly acknowledges the right to wage war, as all treaties now do, according to Kant, is nothing more than a truce. An individual war may be ended, but not the *state of war;* so that, even after cessation of hostilities, there will be constant fear of their renewal, while the armaments known as Peace Establishments will tend to provoke them. All this should be changed, and nations should form one comprehensive Federation, which, receiving other nations within its fold, will at last embrace the civilized world; and such, in the judgment of Kant, was the irresistible tendency of nations. To a French poet we are indebted for the most suggestive term, "United States of Europe"; but this is nothing but the Federation of the illustrious German philosopher. Nor was Kant alone among his great contemporaries. That other philosopher, Fichte, whose name at the time was second only to that of Kant, in his "Groundwork of the Law of Nature" (*Grundlage des Naturrechts*), published in 1796, also urges a Federation of Nations, with an established tribunal to which all should submit. Much better for civilization, had the King at Königsberg, instead of brandishing his gigantic sword, hearkened to the voice of Kant, renewed by Fichte.

With these German oracles in its support, the cause cannot be put aside. Even in the midst of war, Philosophy will be heard, especially when she speaks words of concurring authority that touch a chord in every heart. Leibnitz, Kant, and Fichte, a mighty triumvirate of intelligence, unite in testimony. As Germany, beyond any other nation, has given to the idea of Organized Peace the warrant of philosophy, it only remains now that it should insist upon its practical application. There should be no delay. Long enough has mankind waited while the river of blood flowed on.

UPRISING OF WORKING-MEN.

The working-men of Europe, not excepting Germany, respond to the mandate of Philosophy, and insist that the War System shall be abolished. At public meetings, in formal resolutions and addresses, they have declared war against War, and they will not be silenced. This is not the first time in which working-men have made themselves heard for international justice. I cannot forget, that, while Slavery was waging war against our nation, the working-men of Belgium in public meeting protested against that precocious Proclamation of Belligerent Rights by which the British Government gave such impulse to the Rebellion; and now, in the same spirit, and for the sake of true peace, they declare themselves against that War System by which the peace of nations is placed in such constant jeopardy. They are right; for nobody suffers in war as the working-man, whether in property or in person. For him war is a ravening monster, devouring his substance, and changing him from citizen to military serf. As victim of the War System he is entitled to be heard.

The working-men of different countries have been organizing in societies, of which it is difficult at present to tell the number and extent. It is known that these societies exist in Germany, France, Spain, Italy, and England, as well as in our own country, and that they have in some measure an international character. In France, before the war, there were 433,785 men in the organization, and in Germany 150,000. Yet this is but the beginning.

At the menace of the present war, all these societies were roused. The society known as the International Working-Men's Association, by their General Council, issued an address, dated at London, protesting against it as "a war of dynasties," denouncing Louis Napoleon as an enemy of the laboring classes, and declaring the war plot of 1870 but an amended edition of the *coup d'état* of 1851. The address then testifies generally against war, saying, —

"They feel deeply convinced, that, whatever turn the impending horrid war may take, *the alliance of the working classes of all countries will ultimately kill war.*"

At the same time the Paris branch of the International Association put forth a manifesto addressed "To the working-men of all nations," from which I take these passages: —

"Once more, on the pretext of the European equilibrium, of national honor, the peace of the world is menaced by political ambitions. French, German, Spanish workmen! *let our voices unite in one cry of reprobation against war!* .... War for a question of preponderance, or a dynasty, can, in the eyes of working-men, be nothing but a criminal absurdity. In answer to the warlike proclamations of those who exempt themselves from the impost of blood, and find in public misfortunes a source of fresh speculations, we protest, — we who want peace, labor, and liberty. .... Brothers of Germany! our division would only result in the *complete triumph of despotism on both sides of the Rhine.* .... Working-men of all countries! whatever may, for the present, become of our common efforts, we, the members of the International Working-Men's Association, who know of no frontiers, we send you, as a pledge of indissoluble solidarity, the good wishes and the salutations of the working-men of France."

To this appeal, so full of truth, touching to the quick the pretence of balance of power and questions of dynasty as excuses for war, and then rising to "one cry of reprobation against war," the Berlin branch of the International Association replied: —

"We join with heart and hand in your protestation. .... Solemnly we promise that neither the sound of the trumpet nor the roar of cannon, neither victory nor defeat, shall divert us from our work of the union of the children of toil in all countries."

Then came a meeting of delegates at Chemnitz, in Saxony, representing fifty thousand Saxon working-men, which put forth the following hardy words: —

"We are happy to grasp the fraternal hand stretched out to us by the working-men of France. . . . . Mindful of the watchword of the International Working-Men's Association, *Proletarians of all countries, unite !* we shall never forget that the working-men of all countries are our friends, — and the despots of all countries our enemies."

Next followed, at Brunswick, in Germany, on the 16th of July, — the very day after the reading of the war document at the French tribune, and the "light heart" of the Prime Minister, — a mass meeting of the working-men there, which declared its full concurrence with the manifesto of the Paris branch, spurned the idea of national antagonism to France, and wound up with these solid words: "We are the enemies of all wars, but above all of dynastic wars."

The whole subject is presented with admirable power in an address from the Working-Men's Peace Committee to the working-men of Great Britain and Ireland, duly signed by their officers. Here are some of its sentences : —

"Without us war must cease; for without us standing armies could not exist. It is out of our class that they are formed. . . . . We would call upon and implore the peoples of France and Germany, in order to enable their own rulers to realize these their peace-loving professions, *to insist upon the abolition of standing armies,* as both the source and the means of war, nurseries of vice, and locust-consumers of the fruits of useful industry.

"What we claim and demand — what we would implore the peoples of Europe to do, without regard to Courts, Cabinets, or Dynasties — is *to insist upon Arbitration as a substitute for war,* with peace and its blessings for them, for us, for the whole civilized world."

The working-men of England responded to this appeal, in a crowded meeting at St. James's Hall, London, where all the speakers were working-men and representatives of the various handicrafts, except the Chairman, whose strong words found echo in the intense convictions of the large assemblage : —

"One object of this meeting was to make the horror universally inspired by the enormous and cruel carnage of this terrible war the groundwork for appealing to the working classes and the people of all other European countries to join in protesting against war altogether [*prolonged cheers*], as the shame of Christendom, and direct curse and scourge of the human race. Let the will of the people sweep away war, which could not be waged without them. ["*Hear!*"] Away with enormous standing armies, ["*Hear!*"] the nurseries and instruments of war, — nurseries, too, of vice, and crushing burdens upon national wealth and prosperity! Let there go forth from the people of this and other lands one universal and all-overpowering cry and demand for the blessings of peace."

At this meeting the Honorary Secretary of the Working-Men's Peace Committee, after announcing that the working-men of upwards of three hundred towns had given their adhesion to the platform of the Committee, thus showing a determination to abolish war altogether, moved the following resolution, which was adopted : —

"That war, especially with the present many fearful contrivances for wholesale carnage and destruction, is repugnant to every principle of reason, humanity, and religion; and this meeting earnestly invites all civilized and Christian peoples to insist upon the abolition of standing armies, and the settlement by arbitration of all international disputes."

Thus clearly is the case stated by the Working-Men,

now beginning to be heard, and the testimony is reverberated from nation to nation. They cannot be silent hereafter. I confidently look to them for important co-operation in this great work of redemption. Could my voice reach them now, wherever they may be in that honest toil which is the appointed lot of man, it would be with words of cheer and encouragement. Let them proceed until civilization is no longer darkened by war. In this way will they become not only saviours to their own households, but benefactors of the whole Human Family.

ABOLITION OF THE WAR SYSTEM.

Such is the statement, with its many proofs, by which war is exhibited as the duel of nations, being the Trial by Battle of the Dark Ages. You have seen how nations, under existing International Law, to which all are parties, refer their differences to this insensate arbitrament,—and then how, in our day and before our own eyes, two nations, eminent in civilization, have furnished an instance of the incredible folly, waging together a world-convulsing, soul-harrowing, and most barbarous contest. All ask how long the direful duel will be continued. Better ask, How long will be continued that War System by which such a duel is authorized and regulated among nations? When will this legalized, organized crime be abolished? When at last will it be confessed that the Law of Right is the same for nations as for individuals, so that if Trial by Battle be impious for individuals, it is so for nations also? Against it are Reason and Humanity, pleading as never before,— Economy asking for mighty help,— Peace with softest voice praying for safeguard, — and then the authority of Philosophy speaking by some of its greatest masters, — all reinforced by the irrepressible, irresistible protest of working-men in different nations.

Precedents exist for the abolition of this duel, so completely in point, that, according to the lawyer's phrase, they "go on all fours" with the new case. Two of these have been already mentioned: first, when, at the Diet of Worms, in 1495, the Emperor Maximilian proclaimed a permanent peace throughout Germany, and abolished the "liberty" of Private War; and, secondly, when, in 1815, the German Principalities stipulated "under no pretext to declare war against one another, nor to pursue their mutual differences by force of arms." But first in time, and perhaps in importance, was the great Ordinance of St. Louis, king of France, promulgated at a Parliament in 1260, where he says: "*We forbid to all persons throughout our dominions the* TRIAL BY BATTLE, *and instead of battles we establish proofs by witnesses. . . . .* AND THESE BATTLES WE ABOLISH IN OUR DOMINIONS FOREVER." (Guizot, *Histoire de la Civilisation en France*, Tome IV. pp. 162–164.) These at the time were great words, and they continue great as an example. Their acceptance by any two nations would begin the work of abolition, which would be completed on their adoption by a Congress of Nations, taking from war its existing sanction.

THE WORLD A GLADIATORIAL AMPHITHEATRE.

The growing tendencies of mankind have been quickened by the character of the present war, and the unexampled publicity with which it has been waged.

Never before were all nations, even those separated by great spaces, whether of land or ocean, the daily and excited spectators of the combat. The vast amphitheatre within which the battle is fought, with the whole heavens for its roof, is coextensive with civilization itself. The scene in that great Flavian amphitheatre, the famous Colosseum, is a faint type of what we are witnessing; but that is not without its lesson. Bloody games, where human beings contended with lions and tigers, imported for the purpose, or with each other, constituted an institution of ancient Rome, only mildly rebuked by Cicero, and adopted even by Titus, in that short reign so much praised as unspotted by the blood of the citizen. One hundred thousand spectators looked on, while gladiators from Germany and Gaul joined in ferocious combat, and then, as blood began to flow, and victim after victim sank upon the sand, the people caught the fierce contagion. A common ferocity ruled the scene. As Christianity prevailed, the incongruity of such an institution was widely felt; but still it continued. At last an Eastern monk, moved only by report, journeyed a long way to protest against the impiety. With noble enthusiasm he leaped into the arena, where the battle raged, in order to separate the combatants. He was unsuccessful, and paid with life the penalty of his humanity. But the martyr triumphed where the monk had failed. Shortly afterwards the Emperor Honorius, by solemn decree, put an end to this horrid custom. "The first Christian Emperor," says Gibbon, "may claim the honor of the first edict which condemned the art and amusement of shedding human blood." (Gibbon, Vol. IV. Chap. 30, p. 40.) Our amphitheatre is larger than that of Rome; but it witnesses scenes not less revolting; nor need any monk journey a long way to protest against the impiety. That protest can be uttered by every one here at home. We are all spectators; and since by human craft the civilized world has become one mighty Colosseum, with place for everybody, may we not insist that the bloody games by which it is yet polluted shall cease, and that, instead of mutual-murdering gladiators filling the near-brought scene with death, there shall be an harmonious people, of different nations, but one fellowship, vying together only in works of industry and art, inspired and exalted by a divine beneficence?

In presenting this picture I exaggerate nothing. How feeble is language to depict the stupendous barbarism! How small by its side the bloody games which degraded ancient Rome! How pygmy the one, how colossal the other! Would you know how the combat is conducted? Here is the briefest picture of the arena by a looker-on: —

"Let your readers fancy masses of colored rags glued together with blood and brains, and pinned into strange shapes by fragments of bones. Let them conceive men's bodies without heads, legs without bodies, heaps of human entrails attached to red and blue cloth, and disembowelled corpses in uniform, bodies lying about in all attitudes, with skulls shattered, faces blown off, hips smashed, bones, flesh, and gay clothing all pounded together, as if brayed in a mortar, extending for miles, not very thick in any one place, but recurring perpetually for weary hours, and then they cannot, with the most vivid imagination, come up to the sickening reality of that butchery."

Such a sight would have shocked the Heathen of Rome. They could not have looked on while the brave gladiator was thus changed into a bloody hash; least of all could they have seen the work of slaughter done by machinery. Nor could any German gladiator have written the letter I proceed to quote from a German soldier: —

"I do not know how it is, but one wholly forgets the danger one is in, and thinks only of the effect of one's own bullets, rejoicing, like a child, at the sight of the enemy falling like skittles, and having scarcely a compassionate glance to spare for the comrade falling at one's side. One ceases to be a human being, and turns into a brute, a complete brute."

Plain confession! And yet the duel continues. Nor is there death for the armed man only. Fire mingles with slaughter, as at Bazeilles. Women and children are roasted alive, filling the air with suffocating odor, while the maddened combatants rage against each other. All this is but part of the prolonged and various spectacle, where the scene shifts only for some other horror. Meanwhile the sovereigns of the world sit in their boxes, and the people everywhere occupy the benches.

PERIL FROM THE WAR SYSTEM.

The duel now pending teaches the peril from continuance of the present system. If France and Germany can be brought so suddenly into collision on a mere pretext, what two nations are entirely safe? Where is the talisman for their protection? None, surely, except Disarmament, which, therefore, for the interest of all nations, should be commenced. Prussia is now an acknowledged military power, "armed in complete steel"; but at what cost to her people, if not to mankind!

Military citizenship, according to Prussian rule, is military serfdom, and on this is elevated a military despotism of singular grasp and power, operating throughout the whole nation, like martial law or a state of siege. In Prussia the law tyrannically seizes every youth of eighteen, and, no matter what his calling or profession, compels him to military service for seven years. Three years he spends in the regular army, where his life is surrendered to the trade of blood. Then for four years he passes to the Landwehr, or militia, where he is subject to periodic military drills; then for nine years longer to the Landsturm, with liability to service in case of war until fifty. Wherever he may be in foreign lands his military duty is paramount.

But if this system be good for Prussia, then must it be equally good for other nations. If this economical government, with education for all, subordinates the business of life to the military drill, other nations will find too much reason for doing the same. Unless the War System is abandoned, all must follow the successful example, while the civilized world becomes a busy camp, with every citizen for a soldier, and with all sounds swallowed up in the tocsin of war. Where, then, are the people ? Where are popular rights ? Montesquieu has not hesitated to declare that the peril to free governments proceeds from armies, and that this peril is not corrected even by making them depend directly on the legislative power. This is not enough. The armies must be reduced in number and force. Among his papers, found since his death, is the prediction, " Europe will be lost through her military." (Villemain, *Cours de Littérature Française*, Tome I. p. 423, 15me Leçon.) It is the privilege of genius like that of Montesquieu to lift the curtain of the future; but even he did not see the vastness of suffering in store for his own country through those armies against which he warned. For years the engine of despotism at home, they became the sudden instrument of war abroad. Without them Louis Napoleon could not have made himself Emperor, nor could he have hurried France into the present duel. If needed in other days, they are not needed now. The War System, always barbarous, is an anachronism, full of peril both to peace and liberal institutions.

PEACE.

An army is a despotism; military service is a bondage; nor can the passion for arms be reconciled with a true civilization. The present failure to acknowledge this incompatibility is only another illustration how the clear light of truth is discolored and refracted by an atmosphere where the cloud of war still lingers. Soon must this cloud be dispersed. From war to peace is a change indeed; but Nature herself testifies to change. Sirius, largest and brightest of all the fixed stars, was noted by Ptolemy as fiery-red, and by Seneca as redder than Mars, but since then it has changed to white. To the morose remark, whether in the philosophy of Hobbes or the apology of the soldier, that man is a fighting animal and that war is natural, I reply, — natural for savages rejoicing in the tattoo, natural for barbarians rejoicing in violence, but not natural for man in a true civilization, which I insist is the natural state to which he tends by a sure progression. The true state of Nature is not war, but peace. Not only every war, but every recognition of war as the mode of determining international differences, is evidence that we are yet barbarians, — and so also is every ambition for empire founded on force, and not on the consent of the people. A ghastly, bleeding human head was discovered by the early Romans, as they dug the foundations of that Capital which finally swayed the world. That ghastly, bleeding human head is the fit symbol of military power.

Let the War System be abolished, and, in the glory of this consummation, how vulgar all that comes from battle! By the side of this serene, beneficent civilization, how petty in its pretensions is military power, how vain its triumphs! At this moment the great general who has organized victory for Germany is veiled, and his name does not appear even in the military bulletins. Thus is the glory of arms passing from sight, and battle losing its ancient renown. Peace does not arrest the mind like war. It does not glare like battle. Its operations, like those of Nature, are gentle, yet sure. It is not the tumbling, sounding cataract, but the tranquil, fruitful river. Even the majestic Niagara, with thunder like war, cannot compare with the peaceful plains of water which it divides. How easy to see that the repose of nations, like the repose of Nature, is the great parent of the most precious bounties vouchsafed by Providence! Add peace to Liberty,

"And with that virtue every virtue lives."

As peace is assured, the traditional sensibilities of nations will disappear. Their frontiers will no longer frown with hostile cannon, nor will their people be nursed to hate each other. By ties of constant fellowship will they be interwoven together, no sudden trumpet waking to arms, no sharp summons disturbing the uniform repose. By steam, by telegraph, by the press, have they already conquered time, subdued space, thus breaking down old walls of partition by which they have been separated. Ancient example loses its influence. The prejudices of another generation are removed, and a new geography gives place to the old. The heavens are divided into constellations, with names from beasts, or from some form of brute force, as Leo, Taurus, Sagittarius, and Orion with his club; but this is human device. By similar scheme is the earth divided. But in the sight of God there is one Human Family without division, where all are equal in rights, and the attempt to set up distinctions, keeping men asunder, or in barbarous groups, is a practical denial of that great truth, religious and political, the Brotherhood of Man. The Christian's Fatherland is not merely the nation in which he was born, but the whole earth appointed by the Heavenly Father for his home. In this Fatherland there can be no place for unfriendly boundaries set up by any, — least of all place for the War System, making nations as hostile camps.

At Lassa, in Thibet, there is a venerable stone in memory of the treaty between the courts of Thibet and China, as long ago as 821, bearing an inscription worthy of a true civilization. From Eastern story learn now the beauty of peace. After the titles of the two august sovereigns, the monument proceeds: "These two wise, holy, spiritual, and accomplished princes, foreseeing the changes hidden in the most distant futurity, touched with sentiments of compassion towards their people, and not knowing, in their beneficent protection, any difference between their subjects and strangers, have, after mature reflection and by mutual consent, resolved to give peace to their people. .... In perfect harmony with each other, they will henceforth be good neighbors, and will do their utmost to draw still closer the bonds of union and friendship. .... In preserving their limits, the respective parties shall not attack each other in arms, or make any incursions beyond the frontiers now determined." Then declaring that the two must reciprocally exalt their virtues and banish all mistrust, that travellers may be without uneasiness, that the inhabitants of villages may live at peace, and that nothing may happen to cause misunderstanding, the inscription announces, in terms doubtless Oriental: "This benefit will be extended to future generations, and the voice of love towards its authors will be heard wherever the splendor of the sun and the moon is seen. The Pho will be tranquil in their kingdom, and the Han will be joyful in their empire." (Timkowski's Travels through Mongolia and China, Vol. I. pp. 461–468.) Such is the benediction which from early times has spoken from one of the monuments erected by the god Terminus. Call it Oriental; would it were universal! While recognizing a frontier, there is equal recognition of peace as the rule of international life.

THE REPUBLIC.

In the abolition of the War System the will of the people must become all-powerful, exalting the Republic to its just place as the natural expression of citizenship. At St. Helena Napoleon uttered the famous prophecy, that in fifty years Europe would be Republican or Cossack. The fifty years will expire in 1871. Evidently

Europe will not be Cossack, unless the Cossack is already changed to Republican, — as well may be, when it is known, that, since the great act of Enfranchisement, in February, 1860, by which twenty-three millions of serfs were raised to citizenship, with the right to vote, eleven thousand miles of railway have been opened in Russia, and fifteen thousand three hundred and fifty public schools. A better than Napoleon, who saw mankind with truer insight, Lafayette, has recorded a clearer prophecy. At the foundation of the monument on Bunker Hill, on the semi-centennial anniversary of the battle, 17th of June, 1825, our much-honored national guest gave this toast: " Bunker Hill, and the holy resistance to oppression, which has already enfranchised the American hemisphere. The next half-century's Jubilee toast shall be *to Enfranchised Europe.*" The close of that half-century, already so prolific, is at hand. Shall it behold the great Jubilee with all its vastness of promise accomplished? Enfranchised Europe, foretold by Lafayette, means not only the Republic for all, but Peace for all; it means the United States of Europe, with the War System abolished. Against that little faith through which so much fails in life, I declare my unalterable conviction, that "government of the people, by the people, and for the people" — thus simply described by Abraham Lincoln — is a necessity of civilization, not only because of that republican equality without distinction of birth which it establishes, but for its assurance of permanent peace. All privilege is usurpation, and, like Slavery, a state of war, relieved only by truce, to be broken by the people in their might. To the people alone can mankind look for the repose of nations ; but the

Republic is the embodied people. All hail to the Republic, equal guardian of all, and angel of peace!

Our own part is simple. It is, first, to keep out of war, — and, next, to stand firm in those ideas which are the life of the Republic. Peace is our supreme vocation. To this we are called. By this we succeed. Our example is more than an army. But not on this account can we be indifferent, when Human Rights are assailed or republican institutions are in question. Garibaldi asks for a "word," that easiest expression of power. Strange will it be, when that is not given. To the Republic, and to all struggling for Human Rights, I give word, with heart on the lips. Word and heart I give. Nor would I have my country forget at any time, in the discharge of its transcendent duties, that, since the rule of conduct and of honor is the same for nations as for individuals, the greatest nation is that which does most for Humanity.

THE END.

Cambridge : Printed by Welch, Bigelow, and Company.

Printed in Dunstable, United Kingdom